MODERN WC
SONG COLLECTION

MW00562651

R

Accessing Lyric & Chord Sheets Online

For every song in this book, free printable lyric & chord arrangements are available online, written out in the original key. In addition, for guitarists we've included a "with capo" version for songs in which a capo is critical. These arrangements are perfect for worship bands and musicians needing a quick reference chart.

To download these sheets, go to Alfred.com/ModernWorship. The sheets can be saved one by one as needed, or downloaded in full as a .zip file.

Produced by
Alfred Music
P.O. Box 10003
Van Nuys, CA 91410-0003
alfred.com

Printed in USA.

ISBN-10: 1-4706-3594-1
ISBN-13: 978-1-4706-3594-7

Cover Photo: © Marijana Radonjic / Shutterstock

ARTIST INDEX

CONTENTS

10,000 REASONS (BLESS THE LORD)

Words and Music by
MATT REDMAN
and JONAS MYRIN

5

6

Verse 3:

AMAZING GRACE
(My Chains Are Gone)

Words and Music by
CHRIS TOMLIN and LOUIE GIGLIO

12

14

Chorus:

long as life en-dures.__ My chains are__ gone;__ I've been set__ free. My God, my Sav-iour__ has ran-somed_ me. And like a__ flood,_ His mer-cy reigns, un-end-ing_ love,__ a-maz-ing grace._ My chains are__

4. The earth_

decresc.

Amazing Grace - 5 - 4

AT THE CROSS
(LOVE RAN RED)

Words and Music by
ED CASH, JONAS MYRIN,
MATT ARMSTRONG and MATT REDMAN

21

At the Cross (Love Ran Red) - 9 - 5

22

Chorus:

At the Cross (Love Ran Red) - 9 - 6

BROKEN VESSELS
(AMAZING GRACE)

Words and Music by
JOEL HOUSTON and JONAS MYRIN

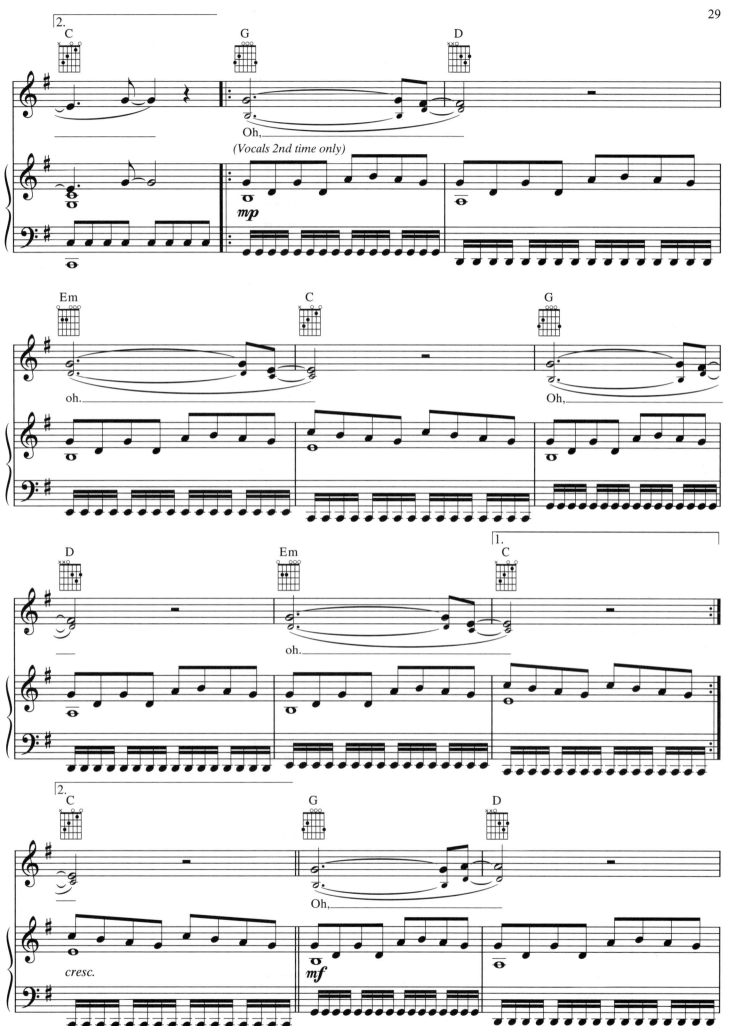

Em
G
D
hand - ed but not for - sak - en. I've been set free, I've been set
heart, Lord; I'll be your ves - sel, the world to see Your life in
Chorus:
Em
D
C
D
free,
me.
A - maz - ing grace, how sweet the sound that
Em
C
saved a wretch like me. Oh, I once was lost but
D
Em
C
now I'm found. Was blind but now I see. Oh, I can see you

32

Chorus:

maz - ing grace, how sweet the__ sound that saved a wretch like__ me.__

__ Oh,_____ I once was lost but now I'm__ found. Was

CHRIST IS RISEN

Words and Music by
MATT MAHER and MIA FIELDES

38

one with Him a - gain. Come a - wake, come a - wake, come and rise up from the grave.____

Verse 2:

2. Be - neath___ the weight_ of all___

___ our sin,___ You bowed_ to none_ but heav - en's will.___ No scheme___

___ of hell,___ no scoff - er's crown,_ no bur - den great_ can hold_

COME AS YOU ARE

Words and Music by
BEN GLOVER, DAVID CROWDER
and MATT MAHER

Slowly, in a passionate worship style ♩. = 45 (♪ = 135)

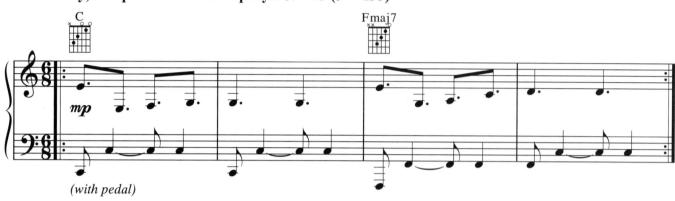

(with pedal)

Verse 1:

1. Come out of sad - ness from wher - ev - er you've been. Come bro - ken heart - ed, let

res - cue be - gin.___ Come find your mer - cy. Oh, sin - ner, come kneel.

Come As You Are - 7 - 1

44

46

EVEN SO COME (COME LORD JESUS)

Words and Music by
CHRIS TOMLIN, JASON INGRAM
and JESS CATES

Even So Come (Come Lord Jesus) - 5 - 1

50

Even So Come (Come Lord Jesus) - 5 - 2

52

CORNERSTONE

Words and Music by
EDWARD MOTE, ERIC LILJERO,
JONAS MYRIN and REUBEN MORGAN

Cornerstone - 8 - 1

Verse 2:

2. When dark-ness comes to hide His face, I rest on His un-

chang-ing grace. In ev-'ry high and storm-y gale,

my an-chor holds with-in the veil.

My an-chor holds with-in

cresc.

the veil.

Chorus:

Christ a - lone, Cor - ner -

f

trum - pet sound, oh, may I then in Him be found.

Dressed in His righ - teous - ness a - lone, fault - less stand be - fore_____ the throne._

Bridge:

EVER BE

Words and Music by
BOBBY STRAND, CHRIS GREELY,
GABRIEL WILSON and KALLEY HEILIGENTHAL

Slowly ♩ = 69

(with pedal)

*Optional: Play cue notes 2nd time.

Oh.

Oh.

Verse:

1. Your love is de-vot-ed like a ring of sol-id gold,
2. You fa-ther the or-phan, Your kind-ness makes us whole.

like a vow that is test-ed, like a cov-e-nant of old.
And You shoul-der our weak-ness, and Your strength be-comes our own.

mf

Ever Be - 7 - 1

64

*Harmony vocals 2nd time.

Ever Be - 7 - 3

68

lips,   ev - er be   on___ my   lips.   Your praise   will___   ev - er   be   on___ my

lips,   ev - er be on my___ lips._____

GREAT ARE YOU LORD

Words and Music by
DAVID LEONARD, JASON INGRAM
and LESLIE JORDAN

Great Are You Lord - 5 - 1

Bridge:

And all the earth will shout Your praise. Our

mp — f

* Use cue notes 2nd and 3rd time.

hearts will cry, these bones will sing, "Great

are You,_____ Lord!"_____ And

Chorus:

It's Your breath in our lungs, so we

FOREVER

Words and Music by
BRIAN JOHNSON, CHRISTA BLACK GIFFORD,
GABE WILSON, JENN JOHNSON,
JOEL TAYLOR and KARI JOBE

Worshipful ballad ♩ = 72

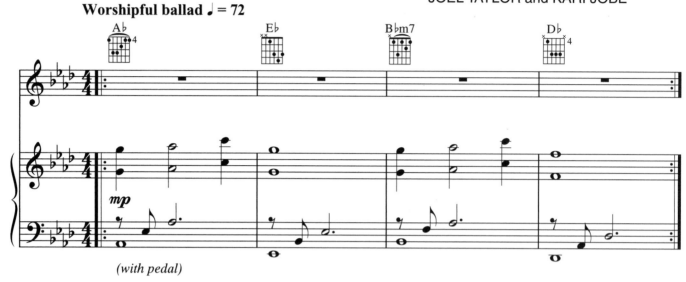

(with pedal)

Verse:

1. The moon and stars, they wept. The morn-ing sun was
2. One fi-nal breath He gave as heav-en looked a-

dead. The Sav-ior of the world was fall - en. His bod-y on the
way; the Son of God was laid in dark - ness. A bat-tle in the

*Play cue notes 2nd time.

cross, His blood poured out for us, the weight of ev - 'ry curse up - on_____ us.
grave, the war on death was waged; the pow'r of hell for -

ev - er_____ bro - ken. The ground be - gan to shake, the stone was rolled a -

way. His per - fect love could not be o - ver - come. Now death, where is your

Forever - 8 - 2

78

Bridge:
A♭ E♭ Fm
We sing hal - le - lu - jah! We sing hal - le - lu - jah! We sing hal - le - lu -
mp
D♭ A♭ E♭
jah! The Lamb has o - ver - come. We sing hal - le - lu - jah! We sing hal - le - lu -
Fm D♭ A♭
jah! We sing hal - le - lu - jah! The Lamb has o - ver - come. We sing hal - le - lu -
E♭ Fm7 D♭
jah! We sing hal - le - lu - jah! We sing hal - le - lu - jah! The Lamb has o - ver - come.

Chorus:

GOOD GOOD FATHER

Words and Music by
ANTHONY BROWN and PAT BARRETT

HOLY SPIRIT

Words and Music by
KATIE TORWALT and BRYAN TORWALT

Moderately slow ♩ = 72

(with pedal)

Verses 1 & 3:

1.3. There's noth - ing worth more____ that could ev - er come close.____

**Use cues notes 2nd time   *Harmony vocals 2nd time.

Holy Spirit - 7 - 1

94

I AM NOT ALONE

Words and Music by
AUSTIN DAVIS, BEN DAVIS,
DUSTIN SAUDER, GRANT PITTMAN,
KARI JOBE, MARTY SAMPSON and MIA FIELDS

I Am Not Alone - 7 - 1

I Am Not Alone - 7 - 5

HOW GREAT IS OUR GOD

Words and Music by
JESSE REEVES, CHRIS TOMLIN
and ED CASH

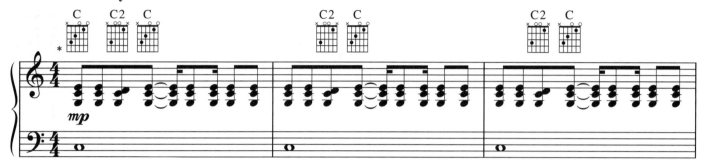

Verse 1 (sing 1st time only):

Guitar cont. simile

1. The splen-dor of____ the King,____

Verse 2 (sing 2nd time only):

age to age,____ He stands,____ and

(play l.h. 2nd time)

clothed in maj-es-ty;____ let all the earth_ re-joice,____ all the earth_ re-joice._

time is in____ His hands;____ Be-gin-ning and_ the End,____ Be-gin-ning and_ the End._

*Original recording in D♭ major with Guitar Capo 1.

IN CHRIST ALONE

Words and Music by
STUART TOWNEND
and KEITH GETTY

In Christ Alone - 5 - 1

IN THE RIVER

Words and Music by
CHRIS QUILALA, JOSHUA SILVERBERG,
MARK ALAN SCHOOLMEESTERS
and RYAN WILLIAMS

Verses 2 & 3:

2. There is a cur-rent stir-ring deep in-side,___ it's o-ver-flow-ing from the heart of___ God,___ the flood of heav-en crash-ing o-ver___ us.___ The tide is ris-ing, ris-ing. Burst - ing, burst - ing up from___ the ground,

116

IT IS WELL

Words and Music by
KRISTENE DiMARCO

122

It Is Well - 8 - 3

126

It is well, it is well with my soul. It is well, it is well with my soul.

And through it

It Is Well - 8 - 7

LORD, I NEED YOU

Words and Music by
CHRISTY NOCKELS, DANIEL CARSON,
JESSE REEVES, KRISTIAN STANFILL
and MATT MAHER

Lord, I Need You - 5 - 1

Chorus:

NO LONGER SLAVES

Words and Music by
BRIAN JOHNSON, JOEL CASE, and
JONATHAN DAVID HELSER

No Longer Slaves - 7 - 5

138

MIGHTY TO SAVE

Words and Music by
REUBEN MORGAN
and BEN FIELDING

* The original recording is in F# major. This arrangement is raised a 1/2 step to G major, to provide a simpler key.
**Play cue notes in left hand 2nd time only.

Chorus:

O COME TO THE ALTAR

Words and Music by
CHRIS BROWN, MACK BROCK,
MATTHEW NTLELE, STEVEN FURTICK,
and WADE JOYE

Moderately slow ♪ = 140 (♩. = 46)

Guitar Capo 4 →

Piano →

(with pedal)

Verse:

1. Are you hurt - ing and bro - ken with - in? _____ O - ver - whelmed _____
2. Leave be - hind _____ your re - grets _____ and mis - takes. _____ Come to - day, _____

_____ by the weight _ of your sin? _____ Je - sus is call - ing. _____
_____ there's no rea - son to wait. _____ Je - sus is call - ing. _____

O Come to the Altar - 7 - 1

148

O Come to the Altar - 7 - 4

150

O Come to the Altar - 7 - 5

152

OPEN UP THE HEAVENS

Words and Music by
MEREDITH ANDREWS, JASON INGRAM,
STUART GARRARD, ANDI ROZIER
and JAMES McDONALD

L.H. tacet first time

Open up the Heavens - 7 - 1

154

Open up the Heavens - 7 - 3

Bridge:

Show us, show us__ Your glo - ry. Show us,

show us__ Your pow - er. Show us, show us__ Your glo - ry, Lord.__

Show us,

C
E♭
show us Your glo - ry.
Show us,
show us Your pow - er.
Em
Gm
Show us,
D
F
show us Your glo - ry, Lord.
C
E♭
cresc. poco a poco
G
B♭
Oh, oh, oh,
C(9)
E♭(9)
We want to see You.
We want to see You.
oh,
oh.

O PRAISE THE NAME (ANÁSTASIS)

Words and Music by
BENJAMIN HASTINGS, DEAN USSHER
and MARTY SAMPSON

O Praise the Name (Anastasis) - 4 - 4

OCEANS (WHERE FEET MAY FAIL)

Words and Music by
JOEL HOUSTON, MATT CROCKER
and SALOMON LIGHTHELM

Slowly ♩ = 64

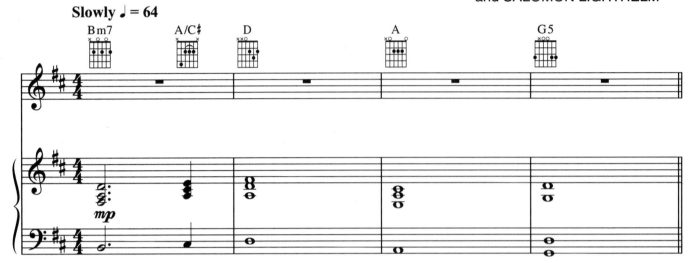

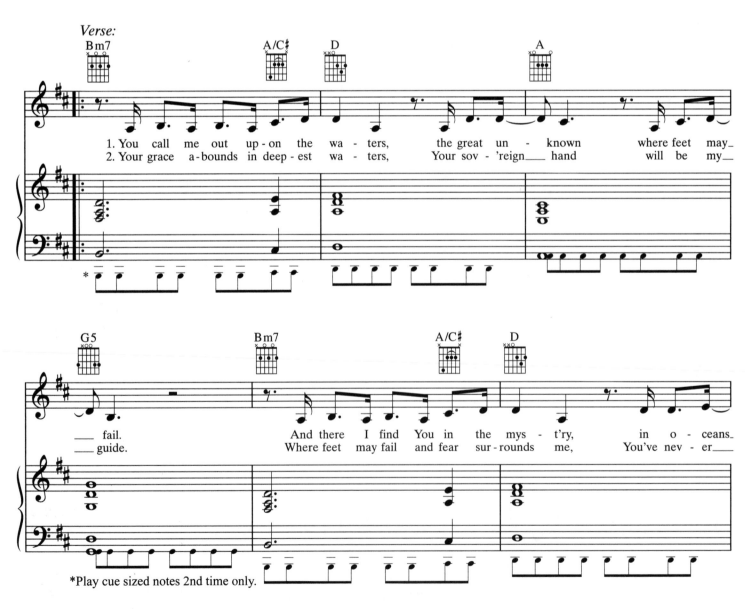

1. You call me out up-on the wa-ters, the great un-known where feet may_
2. Your grace a-bounds in deep-est wa-ters, Your sov-'reign__ hand will be my__

___ fail.
___ guide.

And there I find You in the mys-t'ry, in o-ceans__
Where feet may fail and fear sur-rounds me, You've nev-er__

*Play cue sized notes 2nd time only.

Bridge:

Chorus:

ONE THING REMAINS
(Your Love Never Fails)

Words and Music by
JEREMY RIDDLE, BRIAN JOHNSON
and CHRISTA BLACK

One Thing Remains (Your Love Never Fails) - 8 - 6

One Thing Remains (Your Love Never Fails) - 8 - 8

REMEMBER

Words and Music by
BRETT YOUNKER, DAVID CROWDER,
JOHAN ASGARDE, MATTIAS FRÂNDÁ,
OLIVER LUNDSTROM and SOLOMON OLDS

Remember - 5 - 1

find me. Ho - ly Spir - it,_____ breathe. I've been walk-ing through des - erts.
My prayer: Fa - ther, meet me_____ here. My life for all of Your glo - ry.

I need more of Your pres - ence. I'm weak, Sav - ior, be my_____ strenth.
Your grace, let it sur - round_ me. Let faith change the at - mos - phere.

Chorus:

Down in the_ val - ley when wa - ters_ rise,_ I'm still be - liev - ing hope is a - live.

All through the strug - gle and dark - est day,_ I'll re - mem - ber the emp -

To Coda

ty grave!_

ty grave!_

Bridge:

Hal - le - lu - jah, death is done. All of hell is ov - er - come.

184

RESURRECTING

Words and Music by
CHRIS BROWN, MACK BROCK,
MATTHEW NTLELE, STEVEN FURTICK,
and WADE JOYE

Worship ballad ♩ = 74

(with pedal)

1. The head that once was crowned with

thorns   is crowned with glo-ry now. The Sav-ior knelt to wash our

186

188

Resurrecting - 7 - 4

Verse 4:

sol - diers watched in vain was bor - rowed for three days. His bod - y

there would not re - main. Our God has robbed the_____ grave. Our God has robbed the____

190

Resurrecting - 7 - 6

REVELATION SONG

Words and Music by
JENNIE LEE RIDDLE

1. Wor-thy is the Lamb who was slain. Ho-ly, ho-ly is___ He.___

___ Sing a new song to Him who sits on

194

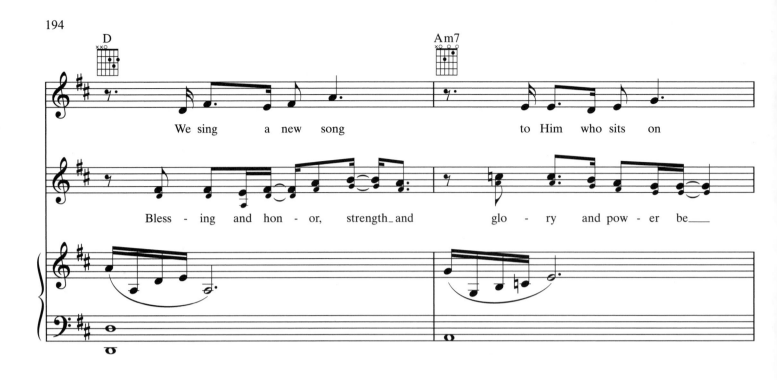

Chorus:

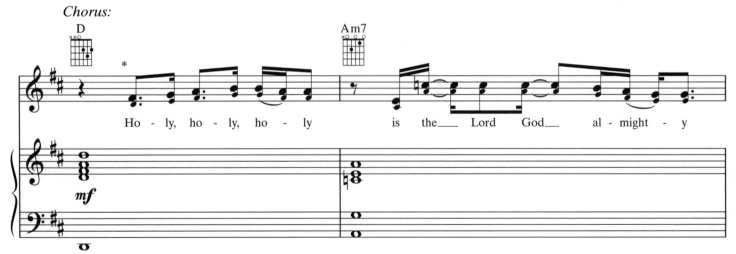

* *Harmony 2nd time only*

Revelation Song - 8 - 3

Chorus:

You a - lone_____ are wor - thy,_____ yeah._____

_____ Ho - ly, ho - ly, ho - ly is the___ Lord God___ al - might - y

who was___ and is___ and is___ to come.___

With all cre - a - tion I___ sing, "Praise to the King of kings;

You are my ev-'ry-thing and I will__ a - dore You.__

I will a - dore__ You."_

Repeat ad lib. and fade

THIS I BELIEVE (THE CREED)

Words and Music by
BEN FIELDING and MATT CROCKER

Verse 2:

Chorus:

This I Believe (The Creed) - 10 - 8

208

THIS IS AMAZING GRACE

Words and Music by
JOSH FARRO, JEREMY RIDDLE
and PHIL WICKHAM

This Is Amazing Grace - 7 - 1

Je - sus I sing___ for all that You've done for___ me.

all that You've done for me.___

Bridge:

Wor - thy is the Lamb who was slain.___ Wor - thy is the King___ who con -

This Is Amazing Grace - 7 - 6

216

Oh,___ Je-sus, I sing___ for all that you've done for___ me.,___

all that You've done for___ me.___

This Is Amazing Grace - 7 - 7

WE BELIEVE

Words and Music by
MATTHEW HOOPER, RICHIE FIKE
and TRAVIS RYAN

Verse 1:

1. In this time of des - per - a - tion

We Believe - 9 - 1

218

We Believe - 9 - 2

Chorus:

220

Verse 3:

let our faith_ be more_ than an - thems,

great-er than_ the songs_ we_____ sing.

And in our weak - ness and_ temp - ta - tions,_ we be - lieve,_

___ we be - lieve._ We be - lieve_

Chorus:

224

Chorus:

WHOM SHALL I FEAR
(GOD OF ANGEL ARMIES)

Words and Music by
CHRIS TOMLIN, ED CASH
and SCOTT CASH

*On the original recording, acoustic guitars play with capo 5.

Whom Shall I Fear (God of Angel Armies) - 7 - 1

228

Whom Shall I Fear (God of Angel Armies) - 7 - 5

232

YOU ARE MY KING
(Amazing Love)

Words and Music by
BILLY JAMES FOOTE

Moderately slow ♩ = 80

(with pedal)

Verse:

I'm for-giv-en be-cause You were for-sak-en. I'm ac-cept-ed,___

You were con-demned.___ I'm a-live___ and well,___ Your Spir-it is with-in___ me be-

cause you died and rose___ a-gain.

You Are My King (Amazing Love) - 6 - 4

238

You Are My King (Amazing Love) - 6 - 6

YOUR GRACE FINDS ME

Words and Music by
JONAS MYRIN and MATT REDMAN

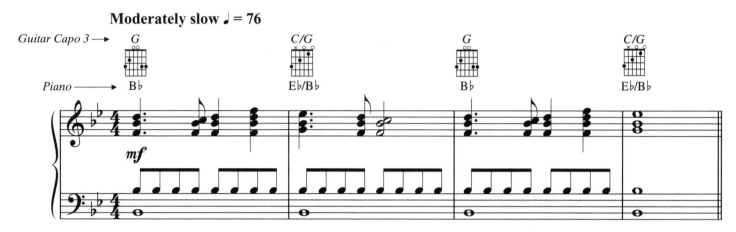

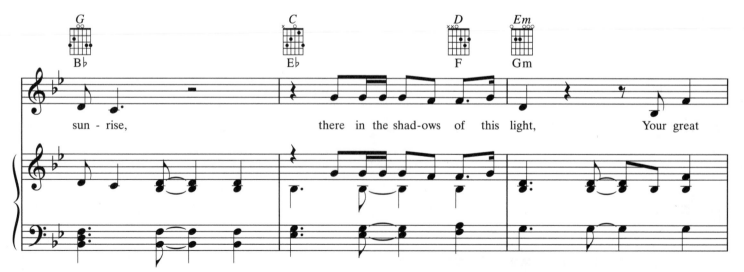

Your Grace Finds Me - 10 - 1

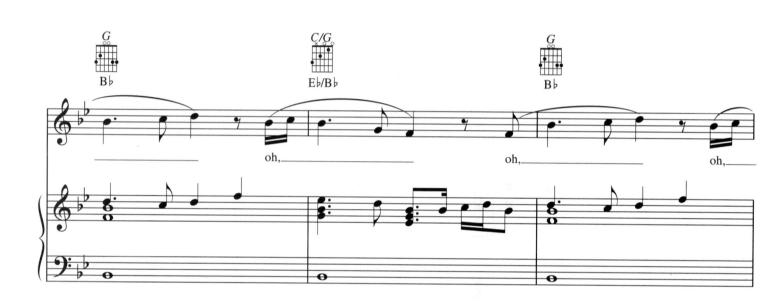

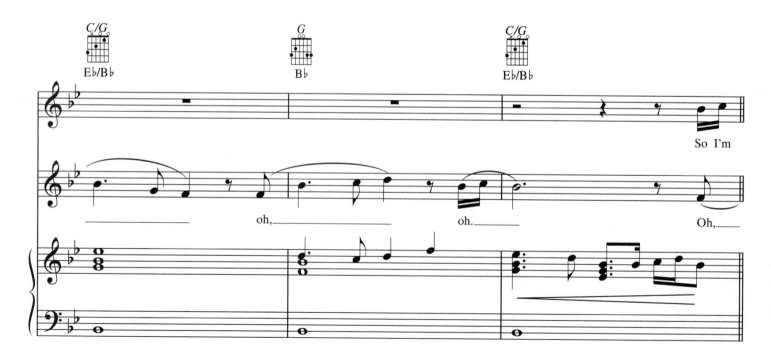

YOUR LOVE AWAKENS ME

Words and Music by
PHIL WICKHAM and CHRIS QUILALA

*Original recording in key of B major.

254